10 Keys to Unlock Your Innovative Self

By Stephen A. Di Biase, Ph.D.

Published by

Premier Insights, LLC
10 E. Ontario Street
Chicago, IL, 60611

www.premierinsightsllc.com

ISBN-13: 78-1511748803
ISBN-10: 151174880X

DEDICATION

To my beloved Denise (Tix) who is my supporter, confidant, best friend and the source of my greatest happiness;

To those mentors who's patience, support and sense of humor encouraged me to embrace change as an opportunity to be innovative.

Contents

Acknowledgments

*"We who have been given much must
give much back to those who follow."*
~ Author Unknown ~

There are many definitions of an innovator. For me, it's a person who embraces change, making something out of nothing in the face of huge obstacles, using little more than their imagination. Our imaginations are most fertile before we clutter our minds with knowledge, arguably around the age of five, when we've learned enough to ask a question but have not learned enough to have an answer.

A simple and actionable definition of innovation is this: *A human response to, and exploitation of, a change that creates wealth in the present.* A cornerstone of the innovative mind is curiosity, because it drives inquiry and seeks understanding that leads to an innovative act, in turn leading to something better. The catalyst driving innovation is the opportunity for a better life. Often, this better life results from the innovator transforming into the entrepreneur.

Those who immigrate to any foreign land, making a life for themselves against all odds, are truly entrepreneurs. I say anyone willing to make the journey, and the

i

sacrifices, are welcome to my home because they're what we want future Americans to embody. Intrinsically, only innovators and entrepreneurs will risk leaving their homes for a better life. They should always be welcomed.

My grandfather emigrated from Italy to the United States in 1920, right after World War I, without resources or language skills, and with my grandmother in tow. They had seven children, all of whom became successful professionals. My grandpa was the "Chairman of the Board" for the "Family Enterprise," but my grandma was the "CEO" who focused on getting results that improved the life of the family. Together, my grandparents, and my parents who followed, made it clear that being an entrepreneur is all about getting results, something I learned early from these generous teachers.

Beyond family, I've had the privilege of spending my youth with some of the most innovative and entrepreneurial people imaginable. I learned much from watching them become successful business people with essentially no formal education. The thought of obtaining a business degree, let alone an MBA, simply wasn't a possibility. These entrepreneurs learned by watching and by doing what those who came before them did to be successful, similar to apprenticing with a master. They taught me much by their examples.

My high school chemistry teacher owned a chain of successful dry cleaning facilities and taught me about the interface of technology and business. As a teen I worked for an Italian baker who invested 50 years of his life building an enterprise. He taught me much by his example of loving his customers. Reaching the workforce after graduate school, and while the topics of innovation and entrepreneurship were still embryonic, my exposure to those who simply innovated out of need and passion was significant. It is to these Masters I owe much.

Once in the real world, I watched other Masters innovate and build businesses where judgment-based decision-making was excellent. There weren't troves of data, and what was available was always too little or too late to be useful.

The lesson learned is that a little knowledge combined with purpose, imagination, curiosity, passion, determination, and judgment will allow someone to be both an innovator and entrepreneur, creating wealth for the many they touch.

I also learned there is no recipe for innovation or entrepreneurship. It's hard but pleasurable work, and very situational. I also learned that successful entrepreneurs and innovators are attentive and observant of opportunities, taking advantage of those opportunities to make their own luck.

Finally, I am blessed that these many generous and effective mentors helped me avoid many of the common, and sometimes fatal, errors that befall the inexperienced. These selfless professionals put up with my immaturity and ignorance because they saw more in me than I could see in myself. They deserve the greatest credit for anything I have accomplished. Without this select group of humanitarians I would have failed for sure.

For anyone who has benefited like me, it's our responsibility to give back to those who follow, which is the main driver for writing this book. I share some of this learning in order to enlighten and catalyze the thinking of the next generation of successful innovators and entrepreneurs.

I've explicitly left all of my many mentors anonymous because it would be unfair to single out the few among the many who were there for me. Being the kind of mentors I envy, they would prefer to be anonymous because what counts most is doing good for its own sake, without any expectation of return or recognition.

Preface

Innovation is like the weather: It's widely discussed and poorly understood, but also critically important. Much has been written about how innovation drives competitiveness, be it as a person, community, business, or country, and how it is critical to increasing our quality of life.

The innovation process, however, is plagued with uncertainty, risk, surprise, and failure. For US-based companies, more than 90% of all innovation initiatives are either abandoned or fail, costing Fortune 1,000 firms alone nearly $80 billion per year. This nationwide view can be applied to any of us, or perhaps all of us.

Fortunately, the innovation process doesn't have to be a chance occurrence or a random event that is contingent upon serendipity or luck. There is a better way, but it requires people to think differently about innovation.

It's clear that only humans can innovate and that innovation really can be taught, learned, and mastered like any discipline. In fact, it can be as easy as learning to ride a bicycle – and once learned it's never forgotten. Most importantly, it's clear that our educational system is perfectly designed to *destroy* a person's natural tendency to innovate (more on that later).

My approach in writing this book is to break innovation down into easy-to-understand and easy-to-use ideas. My hypothesis is simple:

- Everyone is capable of being (and *desires* to be) innovative.
- Innovative behaviors can and must be *taught even before birth*, and then mastered over a lifetime.
- Once mastered, innovative behaviors become a *discipline* never forgotten.
- Innovators and problem solvers are *synonymous*, so teaching people to be innovative empowers them to solve their own problems, leading to a more fulfilling life.
- Innovation is *fun* to teach and do.

It's very difficult to argue that innovation is a *bad thing*. A simple Google search of the term *innovation* yields more than 420 million citations in less than 1 second, with most of them being positive.

The basic elements of innovation are simple. First, it's important to realize that all human beings are born with the ability to innovate. Innovation in its simplest definition is a human response to change creating something valuable in the present. Studying Darwin's work suggests that all living entities adapt to change, but only humans can do it intelligently. Furthermore, all innovation comes from some change force we're compelled to respond to in the present.

Once change takes place, only people are capable of intelligent curiosity. That curiosity results in questions that can lead to innovation. What happened? What is it like? Why did it occur? What does it mean? How do I respond? That last question is one of the most important starting points for innovation: What is it like? It leads to a better understanding of the observed change through something they already understand. This I called *learning by analogy*. After this analysis has occurred, innovators let their imaginations run wild as to the possibilities the change presents. The innovator knows not to limit options too soon after the change has been discovered.

Understanding the change, and what it offers, requires the innovator to know the art of asking good questions, which is something I call *effective inquiry*. It involves framing the change and how to respond to it. But effective inquiry is bounded by how an inquirer learns. Do you learn by reading, writing, doing, observing, or some combination of these? Knowing how you learn, when combined with effective inquiry, leads to understanding and knowledge that gives innovators the edge.

Serious and successful innovators know that the path of true understanding is thinking about possibilities, creating a hypothesis, testing it, interpreting the results, and then repeating the process until knowledge is created. This is also known as the *scientific method*, a process proven over the eons for creating knowledge.

Finally, the best innovators selectively follow their passions in a playful way. Combining *passion* and *play* creates synergies for innovative people that lead to major breakthroughs.

A critical risk for all innovative pursuits and innovators are formal educational processes that value memorization over inquiry-driven understanding. In fact, most formal educational processes and institutions punish inquiry wherever it is found. This fact alone explains why innovation and innovators are in short supply.

I can't suggest a solution to the educational risks we all face, especially our children, except to take matters into our own hands and teach our children ourselves, and teach others by our actions, how to become innovative.

I close the book with a description of a very successful educational experiment in Chicago known as The Academy for Global Citizenship (AGC). AGC is a successful educational platform that combines the elements of both public and private schools into a format that meets the needs of inner-city students.

The program has been in place for several years, starting with kindergarten and finishing with high school. The executive director of AGC has convinced the Chicago School District to invest in their approach on a larger scale as a model for what the school system might be in the future. Obviously, the exception does not make the rule, but having a successful example makes it much easier to replicate additional successful experiments.

The AGC example is a counter-balance to the general belief that the formal educational experience in the United States does everything possible to destroy the natural innovative tendencies we all have by squelching inquiry in favor of rote memorization. Unfortunately, the evidence is clear that we do indeed educate our children how *not* to be innovative, and we do it with excellence.

Whether or not The Academy of Global Citizenship's methods promote innovative characteristics in harmony with teaching facts won't be known until its graduates enter the world. I can't wait to see how they all do.

Stephen A. Di Biase

Introduction

Countries and the people living in them depend on innovation for their long-term survival and happiness, yet the innovation process is plagued with uncertainty, risk, surprise, and failure. An important question is this: Does it need to be that way? Fortunately, innovation can be predictable and learned, just like riding a bicycle, and mastered like any discipline. If this is true, then what can busy, over-worked people do to make themselves more innovative? And why do it anyway?

The first step is recognizing that innovation is not an art form or a random event, but rather a critical *process*; a process with specific steps that, if managed properly, will yield innovative people who get innovative results.

The evidence suggests innovation has not been treated as a skill that anyone can learn, especially young children who are more innovative by nature. I'm not advocating a universal recipe for becoming an innovator. That would be a fool's errand. I'm asserting that certain basic elements of innovation can be learned, taught, and mastered, *making innovation a discipline*, especially if it's taught early in life.

So the question becomes how does one synthesize what has been published about innovation, allowing people to acquire an educated point of view useful in teaching themselves innovative behaviors? Put another way, can this complex topic of innovation be simplified so that busy people can use it? My conclusion is yes, and the details are what follow in this book.

Accepting the definition of innovation as being a human response to change creating a desirable quality of life, then everyone can become to be innovators by first learning to recognize change, defining its meaning, and assessing what responses to make and why, which will lead to solving problems we all face in life. A precondition for such a process to work is that innovation must have common features that apply to all circumstances – and it does.

The approach for developing this educated point of view is to combine the thinking of thought leaders in the field of innovation with the experiences of actual practitioners into a holistic framework. This framework begins with a view that defines which change forces should be responded to, why they're valuable, and what specific choices will be made, all supported by specific actions yielding measurable and desirable results.

Most people learn from their own experiences, but then there is a smaller population who can learn from the experiences of others by witnessing or by reading about events. These people are wise, but in a way that's based on common sense and easy-to-implement ideas.

My contribution is to synthesize an educated point of view from the great minds in the field such that anyone can become more innovative by just reading this book and pondering how it impacts the way they respond to change. Being innovative is a uniquely human phenomenon, and one that is both challenging and pleasurable.

Innovation is "hard-wired" into everyone's DNA, and is how we all adapt to change. Therefore, anyone can be an innovator in the correct circumstances. Innovation is the providence of everyone, regardless of their journey in life, and independent of their background, education level, or socio-economic status.

Innovation has common attributes that can be defined, and when combined with our own experiences, offer a useful template by which anyone can become more innovative.

What are the critical success factors of an innovator? They're quite straightforward, common-sense, normal activities we all embrace without even knowing it. By recognizing these elements we begin to transform innovative behavior from an art form into a discipline.

The critical elements of innovative behavior are as follows:

1. *Collaborative* – Innovation occurs in groups of people often engaged in playful activities. Rarely do innovations come from people working alone.

2. *Involving many skills* – Innovation occurs when a group of people with different skills come together to respond to a given change. Diversity catalyzes everyone to be more innovative.

3. *Results from trial and error* – Experimentation is the cornerstone of learning, allowing people to respond intelligently to change. Doing something now is better that thinking for too long.

4. *Driven by inquiry* – The natural curiosity of children needs to be reinforced as a way of learning by doing and being opened-minded about what's possible. Innovative people know how to grow old without growing up.

5. *Expanded by imagination* – A child-like imagination is how you can connect unrelated dots in ways that are unexpected and innovative. Children don't allow themselves to be bounded by reality. They create new realities.

6. *The process has to be fun* – For children or adults to be innovative requires a playful point of view that is motivated by the individual's passion and protected by their sense of humor.

What does this mean to you?

1. Only people can innovate because only people can think about the changes they're experiencing and respond accordingly. Innovation requires the ability to think. *You must learn how to think.*

2. This thought process needs to be educated, which means that innovative people have some past experience from which to understand the occurring change. The critical question innovative people ask first is this: "Is the change similar to something that I already understand?" Further, innovation is a *collaborative effort* involving many people all asking, "What is it like?" This leads to collective learning and synergies that generate useful knowledge. *You must have many people sharing similar kinds of experiences, figuring out what these experiences mean, and sharing them broadly. This alone makes the Internet incredibly powerful for transforming humankind for the better (or worse).*

3. Learning must occur in multiple ways by doing, watching, listening, and reading about the occurring change. *People must recognize their preferred way of learning and use this as a tool for creating understanding, allowing them to become innovative. This must especially include a safe environment where questions can be asked fearlessly and without risk of punishment.*

4. Fear of inquiry destroys innovative behavior and innovation itself, but sometimes fear of the change

may be warranted. Some changes are dangerous in a physical way. However, it must be safe to learn from experiences. *Your environment needs to be safe enough to allow and even encourage failure.*

My intent is to describe a simple and actionable framework for how people can harness their imagination, curiosity, and inquiry as pathways for them becoming innovators.

In summary, some of the greatest of innovations have occurred when the innovator was "playing" with something they're "passionate" about.

I propose that becoming an innovator is "child's play" if one considers that humans are at their most innovative when they know enough to inquire (i.e., ask a good question) but not educated enough to have an answer. This condition occurs naturally around the age of 5, but can be cultivated at any age. One of an innovator's greatest secrets is knowing how to "age without growing old," which means looking at the world like a 5-year-old with many years of experience and knowledge.

In *Meaningful Learning with Technology*,[1] David H. Jonassen and his co-authors argue that people do not learn from teachers or from technologies. Rather, people learn from thinking – thinking about what they are doing or what they did, thinking about what they believe, thinking about what

---

[1] http://www.amazon.com/Meaningful-Learning-Technology-4th-Edition/dp/0132565587

others have done and believe, thinking about the thinking processes they use – just thinking and reasoning. Thinking mediates learning. *What kinds of thinking are useful for becoming innovative in the new era of technology?*

Analogical. If you distill cognitive psychology into a single principle, it would be to use analogies to convey and understand new ideas. That is, understanding a new idea is best accomplished by comparing and contrasting it to an idea that is already understood. In an analogy, the properties or attributes of one idea (the analogue) are mapped or transferred to another (the source or target). Single analogies are also known as synonyms or metaphors. In using technologies to represent their understanding, people consistently are required to engage in the comparison and contrast reasoning required to structurally map the attributes of one or more idea to others – that is, to draw an analogy.

Expressive. Using technologies as tools to learn with entails learners representing what they know – that is, teaching the computer. To do so, learners must express what they know. Using different tools requires learners to express what they know in different ways. Technologies can be used to help learners express themselves in writing. Learners can express themselves using a variety of tools, such as databases, spreadsheets, and expert systems, each tool requiring different forms of expression. Technologies can support verbal and visual expressions as well. Contrast these varieties of expressions to those required by state-mandated tests, where the only form of expressions is the selection of answer a, b, c, or d.

Experiential. Experiences result in the most meaningful and "sticky" memories. We can recall with clarity experiences that we have had many years before. The primary medium for expressing experiences is the story. Stories are the oldest and most natural form of sense-making. Cultures have maintained their existence through different types of stories, including myths, fairy tales, and histories. Humans appear to have an innate ability and predisposition to organize and represent their experiences in the form of stories. Learning with technologies engages stories in a couple ways. First, the experiences that people have while using technologies to represent their understanding are meaningful and memorable. Second, people may seek out stories and use technologies to convey them.

Problem-Solving. Using technologies to express and convey learner knowledge all entail different kinds of problem-solving. Learning with technologies requires that people make myriad decisions while constructing their representations. Deciding what information to include and exclude, how to structure the information, and what form it should take are all complex decision-making processes. People also engage in a lot of design problem-solving while constructing their interpretations. They also must solve rule-using problems in how to use software. When learners are solving problems, they are thinking deeply and are engaged in meaningful learning. What they learn while doing so will be so much better understood and remembered than continuously preparing to answer multiple-choice test questions.

Key #1: Everyone is Born Innovative

The best way to teach people is by telling them a story.
~ Kenneth Blanchard ~

Discovery is seeing what everyone else has seen
and thinking what no one has thought.
~ Albert Von Szent-Gyorgy ~

Innovation is taking two things that already exist
and putting them together in a new way.
~ Tom Freston ~

Writing for the Innovation Excellence blog, Matthew Griffin notes, "Children are the ultimate disruptive innovators – fearless and able to clash together weird and strange concepts creating something radically different, but unfortunately as we age we lose our creative edge." Why is that? In part, I believe it has to do with becoming "educated," which destroys natural tendencies to innovate.

So the challenge is this: How do you regain the magic of childhood innovativeness? Changing the educational system, while important, is beyond the grasp of most. *However, you can create your own environment that fosters innovative thinking.* So how is this accomplished?

People are the most innovative of all humans around the age of five because they're intelligent enough to ask a *question*, but not educated enough to have an *answer*.

What happens after age five is that the person goes to school and is taught to give *answers* rather than *ask questions*, and curiosity is extracted from the student for the next twenty years by the process known as *their formal education*. Given that curiosity is the root of innovation, our educational system deprives students of their most valuable trait – the willingness to ask genuine questions driven by their innate curiosity. How ironic is that?

Part of what you need to do to become more innovative is training yourself to avoid jumping to giving answers and focus on asking great questions.

If being innovative is part of our basic genetic makeup, then what diminishes the innovative capacity of so many people? A partial answer is the *benign neglect* we invite into our lives. Instead of being alert and engaged, many people opt to be essentially absent because it's easy, and mostly without immediate risk.

In the days of old, apprenticeships were very successful in passing down knowledge from one generation to the next. It was "learning by doing." In today's age, where vast amounts of knowledge are readily available, we can create a "virtual apprenticeship model," learning by studying the experiences of others.

You have to un-do the comforts of modern life by worrying about the changes you're experiencing.

Disciplines are skills that, once taught, learned, and mastered, enter our toolkit as strengths that can be further developed and exploited. Innovation, when learned and adopted as a discipline, is never forgotten.

What innovators do so well is connecting *"unrelated dots"* because they're not held hostage to their knowledge; they control their biases and are excited about being surprised. This is what master innovators do as well, while using their educated points of view in ways that don't bias their powers of observation. When you're young you're a natural innovator right from the start, but only because you're missing the "educated point of view" that compromises our objectivity.

Innovation is the providence of anyone, regardless of their journey in life, and independent of their background, education level, or socio-economic position. Assuming innovation is "hard-wired" into everyone's DNA, and is how we all adapt to change, then anyone can innovate if they know how to *observe the environment around them.*

You must learn how to observe your environment and learn from it by asking honest questions. How do you do that?

In my experience, the most successful approach with people of all ages is combining interesting "looking challenges" with their everyday experiences. Such activities can greatly improve your observation skills, which are essential for primary source analysis, by building on your natural interests. Critical thinking leading to knowledge requires close observation of important details without losing sight of the bigger picture. Try the following suggestions for sharpening your observation skills:

- Challenge yourself to a "30-second look" using an image such as a photograph, map, or work of art.[2] Give yourself only 30 seconds to memorize as many details as possible without taking any notes. Then hide the image while you record as many observations as you can. It's also useful to do this with a partner or group so you can compare and discuss observations, particularly any conflicting or missing details, before observing the image again.

- Challenge yourself to practice close observational skills by putting together pieces of a map such as the 1507 World Map by Martin Waldseemüller.[3]

- Challenge yourself to observe evidence of the creative process by identifying and comparing differences, however subtle, between draft and final versions of the same manuscript, such as the *Ballad of Booker T* by Langston Hughes. Consider possible edits to vocabulary, style, formatting, etc., to "observe" the creative process.

---

[2] http://blogs.loc.gov/teachers/2011/06/look-again-challenging-students-to-develop-close-observation-skills/
[3] See the map at http://memory.loc.gov/cgi-bin/query/h?ammem/gmd:@field%28NUMBER+@band%28g3200+

Key #2: Change Drives All Innovation

There is nothing permanent except change.
~ Heraclitus ~

Change is the law of life. And those who look only to the past or present are certain to miss the future.
~ John F. Kennedy ~

Without change there is no innovation, creativity, or incentive for improvement.
~ William Pollard ~

One simple, but useful, definition of innovation is *a person responding to change in a way that improves the quality of life.* Another way of thinking about innovation is that innovative people have learned how to be effective problem-solvers. So when challenged with the question of why would a person want to become more innovative, the answer is simple: By doing so, your ensure that you will have a higher quality of life by being independently capable of solving the problems you encounter. This, in essence, is perhaps the greatest gift you can bestow upon yourself. So what about change? How do you learn what to look for and then what to do?

Observation is curiosity combined with asking good questions. First, you need to re-cultivate the natural curiosity you had as a child – everything a child sees, feels and hears early in life is new and therefore interesting – and should generate questions. For example, a classic question is, "Why is the sky blue"? You have to legitimize your own childlike curiosity by accepting that *there are no dumb questions* and by pursuing answers to your questions with enthusiasm, thereby rewarding your own curiosity.

Practice asking open-ended questions, which achieves two objectives. First, it makes asking questions okay because you practice doing it all the time. By constantly practicing how you ask questions, you are learning the art of inquiry. Never criticize the questions that pop into your head. Instead, pursue trying to answer them in positive ways. Key #5 will have more information on this topic.

Finally, realize that there are many ways to observe an experience. A useful expression from business is the idea of viewing something from a "360-degree vantage point." What this means is learning how to observe your experiences from as many vantage points as possible. A "360-degree view" aims for a complete view.

A simple way of thinking about observational learning it is the scientific method, which is unconsciously used by almost everyone. Key #7 will focus on using it.

Key #3: Curiosity is Critical

It is a miracle that curiosity survives formal education.
~ Albert Einstein ~

I think, at a child's birth, if a mother could ask a fairy godmother to endow it with the most useful gift, that gift should be curiosity.
~ Eleanor Roosevelt ~

Curiosity will conquer fear even more than bravery will.
~ James Stephens ~

A person's curiosity is innate and undeniable. What looks like simple children's games are crucial to fostering an adult's love of new ideas and experiences, and the confidence to keep discovering. Curiosity compels us to connect with the world, reaching out and testing its boundaries, establishing where they end and everything else begins. Curiosity in people is linking physical exploration through touching, controlling, and creating with physical and imagined experiences. It's intensely pleasurable; a sensuous adventure that is rooted in discovery, such as the 18-month-old who turns a light switch on and off, over and over again, thereby learning about cause and effect.

Children begin innocently challenging what their parents prefer to gloss over. Their curiosity forces us to see the world afresh and challenges our adult assumptions. Recapturing your childlike curiosity is essential if you want to become a more innovative person.

Curiosity starts with the itch to explore. Babies as young as two months old, when presented with different patterns will show a marked preference for the unfamiliar ones. The instinct to explore grows into an instinct for inquiry. Sometime after their first birthday, children start to point at things, looking up at their parent as they do so. One of the main reasons babies point is to signal interest and say, "I want to know about that – what is it?" Before they are able to speak, they are asking a question with their finger. Whether they keep pointing depends on how their parents react. When babies are given the object they are pointing to, they learn that the function of pointing is getting things. Babies who are told the names of the objects come to think of it as a way of getting answers. What happens if they get neither? They stop pointing.

Asking a question requires an impressively sophisticated mental process. **Harvard professor of education Paul Harris notes,** "The child has to first realize that there are things they don't know... that there are invisible worlds of knowledge they have never visited." They also have to realize that other people, like their parents, are holders of important information, and that language can be used as a tool to pull that information out of them.

Growing up in a curious household radically impacts a person's willingness to question. By the time people from curious households go to school, they have a head start on their peers. Having absorbed more information from their parents, they know more, which means they find it easier to learn more. That makes learning more satisfying for them, which in turn feeds their curiosity. What we experience in those early years plays a pivotal role in determining whether we'll become curious adults.

Your primary task in becoming more innovative is to be curious by adopting the perspective of young children, and remain intensely conscious of what you don't know. **Stimulate your own curiosity by doing the following:**

- Acknowledging the questions that pop into your head instead of just dismissing them.

- Be patient in pursuing answers to your questions, fully exploring what you've observed or thought that made a question pop into your head.

- Practice being as curious as any young child by dismissing your biases.

Key #4: Let Imagination Run Wild

Everything you can imagine is real.
~ Pablo Picasso ~

The true sign of intelligence is not knowledge but imagination.
~ Albert Einstein ~

Imagination is something we should all favor. Many experts unanimously celebrate the benefits of a healthy imagination. A person with a good imagination is happier, more alert, better able to cope with life, and more likely to grow into a well-adjusted, secure adult.

Cultivating your own imagination is a great way of putting yourself on the path to becoming a more innovative person.

Sunbridge College's director of teacher-education programs Eugene Schwartz notes the following: "Being a creative adult doesn't necessarily mean you're a painter or sculptor. CEOs and political leaders, too, benefit from being creative, which lets them see things in new ways and find solutions to problems others might miss. That kind of problem-solving and innovative thinking begins with the power of imagination."[4]

---

[4] http://www.parenting.com/article/10-easy-ways-to-fire-your-childs-imagination-21354373

How do we inspire our imaginations? Schwartz's advice is to start with the following basics:

Tell stories. Storytelling may well be the cornerstone of imaginative development, and doing it well and in a variety of ways is something you can do almost every day – even if it is only in brief moments. Great storytellers expand what they observe by imagining what might have occurred, may still occur, or should have occurred because of a change force. This empowers the innovator to expect the unexpected they imagined.

Make art. Tactile experiences are important, and giving yourself free rein over your own creative work is crucial. Engage in painting, drawing, molding, building, or sculpting, but don't force an outcome you want. Let yourself imagine the outcome using a physical medium. Not everyone can "make art" in the physical sense, but everyone can use words to describe something creative using their imagination informed by their unique experiences. Linking the physical, tactical world with our intellect allows everyone to have a "tactical artistic experience," albeit it in a metaphysical way.

Use natural or generic materials. Keeping in touch with objects around us inherently inspires your imagination. Don't dismiss even the simplest elements of your environment. Observe them. Examine them as if you're experiencing them for the first time. Embrace them as if you were 5 years old (or younger). If you watch a toddler experience something new, they do so by looking at it, touching it, smelling it, and then TASTING IT. Young children are always putting new things in their mouths. Why? Because it creates an enduring imprint of what it is. Obviously, tasting the wrong thing could also kill you, which is why good parents carefully manage how their children learn by tasting.

Another technique is tinkering with things that can take an almost infinite number of forms such as blocks or sand. Playing with items that liberate our boundary conditions stimulates imaginative thought.

Foster a sense of inner space. Limit your exposure to media! I know this one sounds crazy in today's media-saturated world, but it's necessary. If all you do is *consume* what others have produced, you lose the sense of inner space needed to *create*, which is an essential part of innovation. Use media as a source of new, and valid forms of data, information, and knowledge to expand your "inner space" without "polluting" it.

Key #5: Learn Effective Inquiry

Inquiry is fatal to certainty.
~ Will Durant ~

It is better to know some of the questions than all of the answers.
~ James Thurber ~

The wise man doesn't give the right answers, he poses the right questions.
~ Claude Levi-Strauss ~

All people are curious, and curiosity is the root of innovative behaviors. Interestingly, most people are unaware of the amazing power of questions in cultivating their natural curiosity, building on their innate innovative abilities. The problem is how parents, and the educational system, strive for answers, which is exactly opposite to what is required for becoming more innovative.

This begs the question: How do you become an effective inquirer? First, there are consequences to *not* asking questions or pursuing answers to the questions that inevitably pop into your head. Consider the following:

- The Titanic sank because planners failed to raise reservations about its design and the steel used to build it.

- Similarly, the Challenger space shuttle disaster was avoidable if the engineers would have questioned the outside temperature at the time of launch. They knew the O-rings were unreliable below 53 degrees Fahrenheit, but they allowed the launch to occur when the temperature was 36 degrees Fahrenheit because they we're fearful of raising the issue since the launch was already well behind schedule.

- A final example is the Bay of Pigs invasion where "Group Think" led to disaster despite many involved having doubts. The thought was if everyone agrees, "They must be right and I'm wrong."

Begin by creating your own safe environment for asking questions. Inquiry-safe environments are those where all questions are addressed seriously, yielding answers and thereby preserving self-esteem, which encourages you to be fearless about inquiry.

Why do people have so much difficulty asking questions? There appear to be many reasons for this, with the following four standing out:

- **We desire to protect ourselves** – People often avoid asking questions to preserve self-image and the image they have in the eyes of others. Basically, they want to avoid "looking dumb." If you don't have the answers, it's better to remain silent and not affirm your "ignorance." To overcome this fear, you must develop confidence and courage, the first step of which is to admit you *don't* know everything (and no one else does either). Education is the goal of asking questions.

- **We are often in a rush** – Everyone is so busy that "there's no time for questions, just action." We just don't take the time to get the best answer. By asking questions, we slow down the pace and increase the quality of the results of our actions. Poor decisions are often worse than not deciding, and the willingness to address ignorance, confusion, and risk through effective inquiry is at the heart of being innovative.

- **We lack the skills in asking** – Good inquiry requires skills not often thought of as critical to life and therefore dismissed or ignored. Asking good questions requires two critical skills: Knowing *what* question to ask (not all questions are created equal) and knowing *how* to ask them.

- **We find ourselves in a culture that discourages inquiry** – Your environment, or culture, determines what kind of personal behavior is acceptable. American culture drives people towards a "rush to action" because contemplation and reflection are seen as weaknesses.

The Art of Asking Questions

Grasping the art of questioning can lead to impressive results. Asking inappropriate questions usually closes off learning. A question asked at the right time and manner, with the right person, is just as important as the content of the question itself.

Great questions are empowering, selfless and supportive, insightful and challenging, and when asked effectively create learning and demand listening. Poor questions are often disempowering, clever in such a way as to deceive those involved, and often judgmental, destroying learning that comes from discovery. So how does one ask great questions? At their root, great questions have several common elements. They do the following:

- Challenge taken-for-granted assumptions.
- Enable people to better view the situation.
- Cause people to explore their behaviors.
- Are open-ended to elicit discussion.
- Generate courage and confidence.
- Lead to positive and powerful action.

There are several types of great questions, including the following:

- Empowering – Focus on positive outcomes.
- Open-Ended – Asking why (5 times).
- Explorative – Have you thought of...?

- Affective – How do you feel about...?
- Reflective – What do you think of...?
- Probing – Describe this in more detail...?
- Fresh – Why must it be this way...?
- Clarifying – What specifically do you mean by...?
- Analytical – Why has this occurred...?

There are two general classes of questions: Those that empowering and those that are disempowering. Empowering questions encourage those questioned to begin thinking constructively about solutions, building self-esteem, creating trust and inviting discovery. Honest questions, which don't accuse the individuals involved, respect self-esteem.

Disempowering questions are judgmental, focusing on blame, closing off options and learning, and often damage self-esteem either directly or indirectly. These two kinds of questions differ in subtle ways. It takes practice and skill to ask empowering questions, especially when one is under pressure. A question can be empowering or disempowering depending on how it's phrased. Below are the characteristics of both types of questions:

Disempowering Questions	Empowering Questions
Blaming	Responsibility
Either/or thinking	Both/and thinking
Defends assumptions	Questions assumptions
Debates	Dialogues
Win-lose outcomes	Win-win outcomes
Protective	Curious

Key #6: Know How You Learn

Learning never exhausts the mind.
~ Leonardo da Vinci ~

Tell me and I forget.
Teach me and I remember.
Involve me and I learn.
~ Benjamin Franklin ~

Education is what remains after one has forgotten what one has learned in school.
~ Albert Einstein ~

One very important thing to know is how you learn. Are you a reader or listener, visual or tactical, or a combination of these? Not many people even know that such distinctions exist, or that very few people have more than one primary method of learning. It's something you must know about yourself. The ratio of listeners to readers is about fifty-fifty. The listener who tries to be a reader or the reader who tries to be a listener will not perform or achieve. Very few listeners can become competent readers, and vice versa.

When he was Commander-in-Chief of the Allied Forces in
Europe, General Dwight (Ike) Eisenhower was the darling
of the press, and attending one of his press conferences
was considered a rare treat. These conferences were
famous for their style, for Eisenhower's total command of
whatever question was being asked, and for his ability to
describe a situation or to explain a policy in two or three
beautifully polished and elegant sentences.

Ten years later, however, President Eisenhower was reviled
by his former admirers. They considered him a buffoon.
They complained he never addressed the question asked,
but rambled on endlessly about something else. He was
constantly ridiculed for butchering the King's English in
his incoherent and ungrammatical answers. Yet
Eisenhower had owed his brilliant earlier career in large
measure to a virtuoso performance as a speechwriter for
General MacArthur, one of the most demanding stylists in
American public life.

Eisenhower apparently did not realize that he himself was a
reader and not a listener. When he was Commander-in-
Chief in Europe, his aides made sure that every question
from the press was submitted in writing at least half an
hour before the conference began. As long as that
happened, Eisenhower was in total command. When he
became President he succeeded two listeners, Franklin D.
Roosevelt and Harry Truman. Both men knew this and
both enjoyed free-for-all press conferences. Roosevelt
knew himself to be so much of a listener that he insisted
that everything first be read out loud to him, and only then
would he look at anything in writing. When Truman

realized after becoming President that he needed to learn about foreign and military affairs, neither of which previously interested him, he arranged for his two ablest Cabinet members, General Marshall and Dean Acheson, to give him a daily tutorial, which each delivered in a forty-minute spoken presentation, after which the President asked questions. Eisenhower, apparently, felt that he had to be like his two predecessors. Most of the time he never even really heard the question the journalists asked, and he was not even an extreme case of a non-listener.

A few years later, Lyndon Johnson destroyed his presidency because he was a listener, although he didn't know it. Johnson's predecessor (John F. Kennedy), who knew that he was a reader, had assembled a brilliant group of writers as assistants, such as Arthur Schlesinger, Jr. (the historian) and Bill Moyers (a first-rate journalist). Kennedy made sure that they first wrote to him before discussing their memos in person. Johnson kept these people as his staff, and they kept on writing. He never apparently understood one word of what they wrote. As a senator, Johnson was superb. Above all else, congressmen must be listeners.

Only a century ago very few people, even in the most highly developed countries, knew whether they were right-handed or left-handed. Left-handers were forced to suppress their left-handedness. Few actually became competent right-handers, most of them ended up as incompetent no-handers and with severe emotional damage such as stuttering.

But only one of every ten human beings is left-handed. The ratio of listeners to readers is more like fifty-fifty. Yet, just as few left-handers became competent right-handers, few listeners can be made, or can make themselves, into competent readers, and vice versa.

The listener who tries to be a reader will suffer the fate of Lyndon Johnson, while the reader who tries to be a listener will suffer the fate of Dwight Eisenhower. They will not perform or achieve.

Schools everywhere assume that everyone learns the same way, but nothing could be further from the truth. When students are forced to learn the way a school teaches and that way is different from their own learning style, it makes school pure torture. For example, many excellent writers do poorly in school, and they tend to remember their schooling as pure torture. This is because writers do not, as a rule, learn by listening and reading. They learn by writing. Since this is not the way the school allows them to learn, they get poor grades.

There are 7 primary learning styles:

1. **Visual (Spatial)** – These individuals learn best through pictures, images, and spatial understanding.

2. **Aural (Auditory)** – These individuals learn best through sound and music.

3. **Verbal (Linguistic)** – These individuals learn best through words, verbal and/or written.

4. **Physical (Kinesthetic)** – These individuals learn best through experience and rely on the sense of touch.

5. **Logical (Mathematical)** – These individuals learn best through logic and reasoning.

6. **Social (Interpersonal)** – These individuals learn best through group interaction.

7. **Solitary (Intrapersonal)** – These individuals learn best through self-study.

It is important to note that many people learn well from a blend of learning styles.   Do you learn best through just one of these learning styles or several?

When you ask people how they learn, most of them know it. But when you then ask them if they act on this knowledge, very few do, and yet to act on this knowledge is the key to success, and to not act on this knowledge is to condemn yourself to mediocrity.

The next key attribute to know is *how you work with others*. Some people work best as subordinates. A prime example is the great American military hero of WWII, General George Patton. He was America's top troop commander. Yet, when he was proposed for an independent command, General George Marshall, the Chief of Staff and the most successful talent recruiter in American history said, "Patton is the best subordinate the American Army has ever produced, but he would be the worst commander."

Some people work best as team members, some people work exceedingly well as coaches and mentors, and some people are simply incompetent to be mentors. Another important thing to know about how you perform is whether you perform well under stress, or whether you need a highly structured and predictable environment.

Finally, you need to *know your strengths*. Most people think they know what they are good at. They are usually wrong. People know what they are *not* good at more often, and even then people are more often wrong than right. And yet, you can only perform with your strengths. You cannot build performance on weaknesses, let alone on something you cannot do at all.

For the great majority of people, knowing their strengths was irrelevant as recently as a few decades ago. People were born into a job and into a line of work. The peasant's son became a peasant. If he was not good at being a peasant, he failed. The artisan's son was similarly going to be an artisan, and so on. But now people have choices. You have to know your strengths so you can know where you belong. Keep the following in mind:

Concentrate on strengths. Place yourself where your strengths can produce the best results.

Work on improving strengths. Get consistent and positive feedback on your strengths and where you might make these even stronger.

Eliminate arrogance. Find the right blend of humility and confidence. Intellectual arrogance causes disabling ignorance, especially for gifted people who might become contemptuous of others with less skill. Gifted people need to teach others how to become stronger in their areas of skills and in the process learn how to teach.

Key #7: The Scientific Method Works

The scientific method works outside of science.
~ Anonymous ~

Reason, observation, and experience; the holy trinity of science.
~ Robert Green Ingersoll ~

If you can't explain it simply, you don't understand it well enough.
~ Albert Einstein ~

The scientific method is the backbone of all rigorous scientific inquiry. The scientific method, honed by everyone from the philosophers of ancient Greece to the scientists of today, is a proven method of effective inquiry designed to advance scientific work and further the accumulation of knowledge. While there are some variations on the method and disagreement over how it should be used, the basic steps are easy to understand and invaluable not only to scientific research but also to solving everyday problems.

Teaching yourself the scientific method is a must, and something you'll find natural since it's how our minds are "wired" to operate.

The method involves the following simple steps:

- Recognizing a change has occurred.
- Questioning what the change means.
- Suggesting responses to the change leading to desirable outcomes.
- Implementing the responses and measuring results.
- Assessing the results in creating the next response.
- Then repeating the process.

Learning how to use the scientific method empowers you to deal with the unknowns you experience.

The Scientific Method as an Ongoing Process

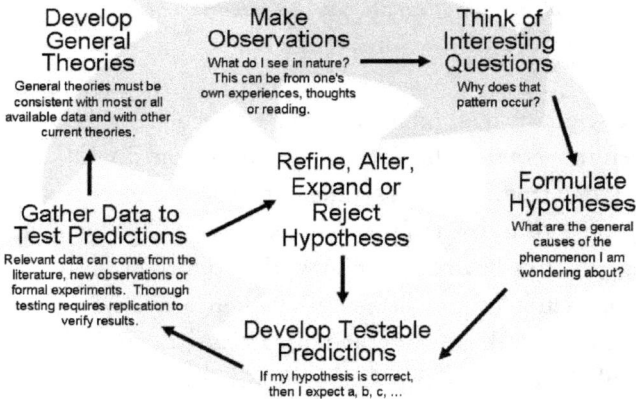

A critical element of the scientific method is that what you observe is measurable, either quantitatively or qualitatively. While quantitative measurements are not always possible, estimating what is observed can usually be done. Being a "good estimator" is a useful tool in the innovators tool box. Estimating the impact, scope, scale etc. of the change your observing is mandatory in recognizing the opportunity embedded in the change that can be taken advantage of creating value – the innovation. Innovators realize initially that "close enough is good enough" yielding something to build upon.

Stephen A. Di Biase

Key #8: Pursue Your Passion

Don't worry about what the world needs. Ask what makes you come alive and do that, because what the world needs is people who have come alive.
~ Howard Thurman ~

Passion is energy. Feel the power that comes from focusing on what excites you.
~ Oprah Winfrey ~

Nothing is as important as passion. No matter what you want to do with your life, be passionate.
~ Jon Bon Jovi ~

It is intuitively obvious that excellence comes from people combining their passion with their strengths. It is common sense that people are passionate about what they're good at, especially when they're recognized for it. If you don't feel like you know what your passions are, here are some questions to help you figure it out:

1. If I had all the time in the world, how would I spend it (don't let potential boundaries stifle your thoughts)?

2. Where do I get, or what gives me, energy and motivation?

3. What do I really care about (people, organizations, relationships, human issues, social issues, etc.)?

4. What was I most proud of this week?

5. What gifts and talents do I have?

6. What inspires and motivates me?

7. Where am I headed?

8. Who do I really want to be?

9. How do I truly see myself? If you're a "work in progress," what does that mean?

10. What are you striving for?

When you figure out what your passions are, you will naturally become more innovative from the creative energy you get from pursuing your passion, especially when you combine it with "child-like" thinking.

Being a "passionate, child-like person" allows the innovator to dismiss their biases about the change they're experiencing and seeing it for what it is and not what they want it to be. When this occurs, especially for a sustained period of time, unexpected, innovative thoughts begin to form.

Combining this with like-minded people (other innovators) often results in a "string of thoughts" that, when stitched together, yields something one person alone can't imagine.

A trick that many innovative people do is writing down their assumptions about the change they're observing and validating these assumptions, creating facts leading to actionable knowledge, and creating value. It's *creating value* that makes something innovative.

Stephen A. Di Biase

Key #9: Play More

You can discover more about a person in an hour of play than in a year of conversation.
~ Plato ~

This is the real secret of life – to be completely engaged with what you are doing in the here and now. And instead of calling it work, realize it is play.
~ Alan W. Watts ~

Humanity has advanced, when it has advanced, not because it has been sober, responsible, and cautious, but because it has been playful, rebellious, and immature.
~ Tom Robbins ~

Nothing is more impactful on developing innovators than play. And while *play* is a simple term, it defies a simple definition, and doesn't fit neatly any single characteristic. Instead, it involves a constellation of characteristics that have to do with the motives, or mental framework, underlying the observed behavior.

Experts conclude that essentially all of the descriptors of human play can be boiled down to the following five:

Play Is Self-Chosen and Self-Directed

Play, first and foremost, is what one wants to do, as opposed to what one feels obliged to do. Players choose not only to play, but how to play, and that is the meaning of the statement that play is self-directed. In social play (play involving more than one player) one person may emerge as the leader, but only at the will of all the others. Anyone may propose rules, but the rules must be agreeable to all if the behavior is to remain in the realm of play for all. The most basic freedom in play is the freedom to quit. Any player will quit the game if the leaders are enforcing rules that are not agreeable with the other players.

Play is intrinsically motivated – means are more valued than ends

Play is an activity done for its own sake more than for some reward outside of the activity itself. In other words, it is behaviors where "the means" are more valued than "the ends." When people are not playing, what they value most are the results of their actions. A person may scratch an itch to get rid of the itch, flee from a tiger to avoid being eaten, or work at a boring job for money. If there were no itch, tiger, or paycheck, the person would not scratch, flee, or work. In play, participants are not necessarily looking for the easiest routes to achieving the ends.

Play is guided by mental rules, but the rules leave room for creativity

Play is a freely chosen activity with boundary conditions. Play always has structure, and that structure derives from rules in the players' minds. All of the players in social play share the rules at least partially. The rule-based nature of play is the characteristic emphasized most strongly, that play is the means by which people learn to control their impulses and abide by socially agreed-upon rules.

The rules of play provide boundaries within which the actions must occur, but they do not precisely dictate each action; they always leave room for creativity.

Different types of play have different types of rules. A basic rule of constructive play, for example, is that you must work with the chosen medium in a manner aimed at producing or depicting some specific object or design that you have in mind. In socio-dramatic play (the playful acting out of roles or scenes, as when children play "house" or pretend to be superheroes), the fundamental rule is that players must abide by their shared understanding of the roles that they are playing; they must stay in character. Even playful fighting and chasing, which may look wild to the observer, is constrained by rules. An always-present rule in children's "play fighting," for example, is that the players mimic some of the actions of serious fighting, but don't really hurt the other person.

Play is imaginative
Play always involves some degree of mental removal of oneself from the immediately present real world. Play provides the engine for cultural innovations. This is the characteristic of play in the development of creativity and the ability to think in ways that go beyond the concrete here-and-now. The imaginative nature of play is, in a

sense, the flip side of play's rule-based nature. For this kind of play, rules in the player's minds, not by laws of nature, govern outcomes.

Imagination, or fantasy, is most obvious in socio-dramatic play, where the players create the characters and the plot, and it is present in other forms of human play. For example, in rough and tumble play, the fight is a pretend one, not a real one. In constructive play, the players may say that they are building a castle from sand, but they know it is a pretend castle, not a real one. In formal games with explicit rules, the players must accept an already established fictional situation that provides the foundation for the rules. For example, in the real world bishops can move in any direction they choose, but in the fantasy world of chess they can move only on the diagonals.

Play is conducted in an alert, active, but relatively non-stressed frame of mind

This final characteristic of play follows naturally from the other four. Because play involves conscious control of one's own behavior, with attention to means and rules, it requires an active, alert mind. Players have to think actively about what they are doing. Yet, because play is not a response to external demands, and because the activity takes place in a fantasy world rather than the real world, and because the ends do not have immediate consequences in the real world, the person at play is relatively free from pressure or stress.

Play can have mental tension arising as players strive to perform well, but since play is always self-chosen, so is any mental tension that accompanies it. If the tension becomes too great, reaching the level of distress, the player is free to quit or change the structure of the play at any time and thereby relieve the tension. If an activity becomes compulsive, so that the person continues at it despite a high degree of mental distress, then the activity is no longer play.

The mental state of play, attuned to the activity itself, reduces consciousness of self and time. The mind, wrapped up in the ideas, rules, and actions of the game, is impervious to outside distractions. This state of mind is ideal for creativity and the learning of new skills.

The some of the material in this section was adapted from the following websites:

- http://www.nifplay.org/
- http://www.scholarpedia.org/article/Encyclopedia:Play_Science
- http://www.scholarpedia.org/article/Definitions_of_Play

Key #10: Beware of Formal Education

It is a miracle that curiosity survives formal education.
~ Albert Einstein ~

Strange as it may seem, no amount of learning can cure stupidity, and formal education positively fortifies it.
~ Stephen Vizinczey ~

Steve Jobs, Bill Gates and Mark Zuckerberg didn't finish college. Too much emphasis is placed on formal education - I told my children not to worry about their grades but to enjoy learning.
~ Nassim Nicholas Taleb ~

In his landmark 1973 book, *The Coming of Post-industrial Society*, sociologist Daniel Bell heralded the US transition from a labor-intensive economy producing goods to a knowledge-based one of providing services. Manual, assembly-line work would give way to work *requiring advanced skills and creativity*. American politicians and pundits have regularly stressed that education holds the key to the country's future. Everyone agrees that good schools are prerequisites for broad economic prosperity, individual social mobility, and a healthy civil society in which informed voters engage in the public issues of the day.

Other countries, meanwhile, have figured out a better way to educate their children; one that looks less like the US education system and more like its professional schools (e.g., medical, law, etc.). Recent international research suggests that the countries with top-ranking education owe their success to approaches that are in many ways the inverse of the American one. Canada, Finland, Japan, Singapore, and South Korea are all top scorers on the Program for International Student Assessment, an internationally recognized test for 15-year-olds that measures higher-order problem-solving in math, reading, and science. And they all do certain things similarly.

They choose their teachers from among their most talented graduates, train them extensively, create opportunities for them to collaborate with their peers within and across schools to improve their practice, provide them the external supports that they need to do their work well, and underwrite all these efforts with a strong welfare state.

Because these countries do a good job of training their educators to begin with, they have less need to externally monitor school performance. If the US wants to lead the world in student achievement, it will need to borrow some ideas from the countries that currently top international rankings. Rather than simply holding accountable the teachers and schools that have failed to live up to expectations, the country will need to build a new system from the ground up – an expert profession that can consistently deliver high levels of performance.

What might a better approach to education look like in the US? One example of a hybrid of a public school/private school and gifted program is found in the case study of the Academy for Global Citizenship (AGC) in Chicago, IL. See the following for more information:

- http://listverse.com/2013/01/20/10-poorly-educated-but-incredibly-successful-people/
- http://www.foreignaffairs.com/articles/139113/jal-mehta/why-american-education-fails
- http://agcchicago.org/school/our-mission/

There are many laudable approaches for improving public education, which can yield confusion between public, magnet, charter, and private school options. The Academy of Global Citizenship (AGC) is a Chicago Public Charter school that enrolls students through a blind public lottery, without tuition or testing students prior to admission. AGC's innovations have come from learning global best practices through observing schools in 90 countries around the world, including public and private schools. It's a classic recombination of things known into something new and innovative. Further, AGC students observe how their education is delivered and are encouraged to imagine how it could be improved. The school itself fosters immersion in the process of innovation.

This is a great example of innovators becoming more innovative by innovating. It's a virtuous cycle that anyone can learn to make innovation a discipline. Not only is AGC teaching the next generation of students how to become innovators by innovating in their school, they're doing it in such a way that it will become part of their normal approach to the world. AGC is making education capable of teaching students to be problem solvers, exactly what the world needs to become a better place.

The full story, of course, is that AGC is a complex ecosystem where curriculum, culture, and community come together to support the growth of the whole child. As an International Baccalaureate World School, AGC teaches through a process of inquiry that begins with an invitation to discuss what we know and would like to learn about a given topic, and ends with action, applying our knowledge to make the world a better place. You can inspect a sample unit of inquiry based learning on their website at http://agcchicago.org/academics/academics-unit-1/ and read about one of my favorite action pieces at https://agcchicago.wordpress.com/2013/04/23/agc-students-march-against-plastic/

Two Examples

Where Does Our Food Come From?
Students engage in a discussion with each other about where their food comes from. They make their thinking visible by charting their brainstorm ideas using a circle map. Following this, students refine their ideas and start to generate questions as they take field trips to a bread factory, an organic food distributor, and a farmer's market. Mathematical concepts of estimating, counting, and measuring are explored as students investigate the size and weight of various vegetables.

Students gain a deeper understanding of food production by learning how to gather information from non-fiction books. Upon introduction to textbook's features including the table of contents, headings, bold words, and glossaries the students retell a series of events in sequence related to food production supported by a written summary. They use vocabulary words such as, first, next, and last.

The class revisits their initial brainstorm circle maps reflecting on what they previously knew about food production, what they learned, and what wonderings they still have. Parents report that their students are asking for unprocessed foods at the grocery store such as 100% juice and whole grain bread. The staff observes students choosing to interact with the school garden at recess: Students are eager to notice the changes that happen each day.

AGC Students Marching Against Plastic – An Example of Early Activism!

As part of a six-week unit of inquiry called *Our Global Impact*, AGC fourth graders learned about how human behaviors and actions negatively affect the environment. Students, inspired by their research, evaluated various courses of action for reducing the negative impact of plastic bags on their planet. After watching the documentary *Bag It*, they were inspired to do some investigative journalism of their own. They invited Coleman Franklin, Co-founder and Vice President of Better Bag, and conducted an interview on camera. Coleman and his colleagues are part of a statewide and national movement to ban plastic bags because of their profound effect on the environment, the food chain, and human health. Better Bag, a Chicago-based startup, is offering a plastic bag alternative made out of corn, sugar cane, and other plants.

As they uncovered the truth about plastic, the students were shocked to find out how harmful plastic is to the Earth, the animal kingdom and, ultimately, themselves. In addition to working on their own documentary to raise awareness about plastic and its alternatives, they organized a peaceful protest against the unnecessary use of plastic and plastic bags.

Fourth-graders invited their peers, families, AGC staff, and community members to march from 46th Street to Archer Park on Earth Day, April 22 with signs and slogans, all the while picking up trash, plastic, and compostable items in the neighborhood. Classes from kindergarten to 5th grade were invited, and many voted to join the march. Once at the park, 4th-graders led small group discussions with their peers to share with them what they had learned in their unit of inquiry. They filled the park with colorful posters drawn on recycled paper and cardboard with original slogans such as "Plastic Is Lame" and "Say BOO To Plastic."

Sarah Elizabeth Ippel, Founder and Executive Director of AGC:

"The Academy for Global Citizenship is a Chicago Public Charter School, located on the underserved Southwest side of Chicago. Our innovative and holistic approach to education aims to foster systemic change and inspire the way society educates our future generations. We are producing a replicable model for learning in the 21st century, including the construction of a net-positive energy campus."

Our Mission
AGC develops insightful leaders who take action both now and in the future to positively impact their communities and the world beyond.

Our Vision
AGC will ignite a movement to create a better world. We will transform our educational systems by being an incubator of innovation. Using a foundation of academic knowledge and global-mindedness each student will create a life of possibility and contribute to a more peaceful and just society.

The Academy for Global Citizenship offers a relevant, engaging and challenging educational program for all children. Every child is held accountable for achieving rigorous academic standards. Our inquiry-based learning curriculum provides an opportunity for learners to construct meaning through concept-driven units of study. Students become environmentally and internationally minded by learning how their choices impact their community and ultimately the world. The Academy for Global Citizenship places an emphasis on the total growth of the developing child by addressing social, physical, linguistic, emotional and cultural needs in addition to academic development. As a community of learners; professionals, families, and teachers work collaboratively

to ensure the learning environment supports high
achievement.

*AGC respects and embraces the innate curiosity of children, the
natural systems of the world and the responsibility to make positive
change.*

Our Founder

In addition to studying the application of the International
Baccalaureate framework in various cultural contexts
across the globe, her earlier initiatives included the
development and implementation of globally cooperative
literacy programs for orphan children in northern
Tanzania. Sarah Elizabeth has further completed studies
in Nonprofit Management at Harvard Business School.
During her five-year term as Vice President of Education
on the governing board of the United Nations Association,
Sarah Elizabeth fostered broader implementation of The
Growing Connection, an organic gardening initiative
established to cross-culturally connect children and
educators across continents through technology. She has
also served on the Chicago Chapter of the United States
Green Building Council Green Schools Advocacy
Committee, Chicago Public Schools' Environmental
Action Plan Taskforce, and is an active founding member
of Conservation International's Generation Conservation.
Sarah Elizabeth's additional leadership and civic
contributions have also included executive board
memberships with Northwestern Memorial Hospital and
the Art Institute of Chicago. Sarah Elizabeth was selected
as a United States Delegate to Terra Madre in 2010, where
she met with representatives from over 60 nations to

discuss the sustainability of our local and global food systems. In 2011, she was named one of Monocle's Top 20 International Pioneers in Education alongside Michelle Rhee, and visited the White House to receive a national award from Michelle Obama.

In 2012 and 2013, Sarah Elizabeth was appointed as one of 100 Delegates from 20 countries across the globe that assembled for the G8 Young Global Leader's Summit, preparing recommendations for a communiqué that was presented to President Obama and the U.S. Department of State. In 2013, Sarah Elizabeth was recognized by Forbes as one of the nation's "top five game changers in education", was the recipient of the GOOD 100 list of "people pushing the world forward through doing" and was selected by the Council on Global Affairs as an Emerging Leader Fellow. When she is not traveling around the world, giving TED talks and sharing the Academy for Global Citizenship's vision for systemic change, Sarah Elizabeth enjoys working on her plans to build a net-positive energy home in Chicago.

AGC...

- Is a Chicago Public Charter School with 400 Kindergarten through Seventh Grade students.
- Is located in an industrial, underserved area on Chicago's Southwest side.
- Serves 91% minority and 80% low-income students.
- Opened in August of 2008 with Kindergarten & First Grade.
- Will add one grade level per year to create a continuum of K to 8 International.

- Baccalaureate education within the Chicago Public School system.

AGC develops insightful leaders who take action both now and in the future to positively impact their communities and the world beyond. In pursuit of this mission, AGC is committed to:
- Serving the whole child & facilitating collaboration within the community.
- Modeling academic excellence & developing inquirers.
- Cultivating international awareness & fostering environmental stewardship.

The Academy for Global Citizenship has been:
- Invited to the White House by Michelle Obama to be recognized and the Midwest first and nation's second "Healthier US School," the USDA's highest honor.
- Designated as a National Green Ribbon School by US Education Secretary, Arne Duncan.
- Asked to present to the United States Department of Education on scaling our innovation.
- Authorized by the International Baccalaureate (IB) Organization as an IB World School.
- Provided a Congressional Record from the US House of Representatives.
- Commended by Mayor Rahm Emanuel and Governor Pat Quinn as a model for Chicago.
- Recognized in an array of local, national and international media sources, including the New York Times, Good Morning America, NBC, ABC, Fox News, NPR, Atlantic Monthly, Monocle,

Chicago Tribune, Sun-Times, Univision, and Forbes among others.

I've spent a considerable amount of time on showing you an alternative for how education could happen in schools that would foster instead of kill innovation in students.

If you're planning on furthering your education, just keep in mind that one of its unintended side effects is to stifle innovation. Although this will not be nearly as prevalent in higher education as it is in K-12 schools, it remains something to be wary of in any educational setting.

Conclusion

Children are perhaps the most innovative humans at the age of five because they're intelligent enough to ask a question but not educated enough to have an answer. Your goal of unlocking your innovative self depends in large measure on your willingness to rediscover the magic of childhood that may have been largely educated out of you.

In school a child learns that answers are more valuable than questions, with curiosity extracted from the student by the process known as *"their formal education."* Given that curiosity is the root of innovation, does our educational system deprive students of their most valuable trait, which is the willingness to ask genuine questions driven by their innate curiosity? I'm afraid so.

If being innovative is part of our basic genetic makeup, then what diminishes the innovative capacity of so many people is our educational system combined with *"benign neglect"* of parents. The critical question is this: How can it be reacquired?

People depend on innovation for their long-term survival and happiness, yet the innovation process is plagued with uncertainty, risk, surprise, and failure. An important question is: Dose it need to be that way? Innovation doesn't have to be a chance occurrence, or a random event.

If learning innovation as a discipline is possible, then what does a busy person do to become more innovative, and why bother?

A simple but useful definition of innovation is a person responding to change in a way that improves the quality of life. Another way of thinking about innovation is that innovative people have learned how to solve problems effectively. So when challenged with the question of why people might want to become more innovative, the answer is simple: By doing so, you ensure that you will have a higher quality of life by being independently capable of solving the problems you encounter.

Innovation, while a complex topic, can be understood in ways that anyone can use it to improve their own lives and those of their children. What I've suggested is that innovation can be broken down into the simplest elements that when recombined provide a roadmap for becoming more innovative. This is what I've attempted to do with *10 Secrets to Becoming a More Innovative Person.*

This book explained innovative behaviors in 10 easy-to-understand, usable ideas. My hypothesis is simple:

- Everyone is capable of being (and *desires* to be) innovative.
- Innovative behaviors can and must be *taught before birth*, and mastered over a life time.
- Once mastered, innovative behaviors become a *discipline* never forgotten.
- Innovators and problem solvers are *synonymous*, so becoming more innovative empowers you to solve you own problems, leading to a more fulfilling life.
- Innovation is *fun* to teach and do.

Knowing how to innovate can become a tool for describing well defined and "elegant" solutions for both simple and complex problems. This can be the greatest and longest-lasting gift people can give to themselves.

10 Secrets to Becoming a More Innovative Person outlines a starting point for those who desire to embark on this journey of becoming more innovative. The approach is simple:

- Stimulate your natural curiosity.
- Make your environment a safe place to ask questions.
- Learn how to ask a proper question.
- Test your hypothesis with experiments.
- Repeat the process.

Good luck and Godspeed in becoming an innovative problem solver. Our country and world needs you if we are to meet the challenges ahead.

Bibliography – Articles

1. http://www.forbes.com/sites/dorieclark/2012/08/22/why-innovative-people-fail/

2. https://www.google.com/search?q=innovative+peopl e&sa=X&espv=2&biw=1360&bih=601&tbm=isch&t bo=u&source=univ&ei=3ZMdVbLpD8ueNtLVgugN &ved=0CDEQsAQ&dpr=1

3. https://innovationstyles.com/isinc/content/personal profile.aspx

4. http://www.fastcompany.com/section/most-creative-people-2014

5. http://www.forbes.com/sites/innovatorsdna/2012/0 9/05/how-innovative-leaders-maintain-their-edge/

6. http://www.huffingtonpost.com/soren-petersen/the-power-of-personal-storytelling-in-design-and-innovation_b_6448912.html

7. http://www.baselinemag.com/c/a/Innovation/11-Practical-Ideas-for-Personal-Innovation-395525

8. http://www.triz-journal.com/innovation-theories-strategies/innovation-general/assess-personal-innovation-levels/

9. http://materialise.com/innovation-with-a-personal-touch

10. http://www.innovationmanagement.se/imtool-articles/your-personal-innovation-profile/

Bibliography – Institutes

1. http://www.strategicbusinessinsights.com/vals/u stypes/innovators.shtml

2. http://pfi.dod.mil/

3. http://www.vuvan.com/what-is-personal-innovation/230

4. http://haydnshaughnessy.com/personal-innovation-lifestyle/

5. http://www.aspeninstitute.org/policy-work/communications-society/power-curve-society-future-innovation-opportunity-social-equity

6. http://www.christenseninstitute.org/key-concepts/disruptive-innovation-2/

7. http://www.debaak.com/about-you/challenges/innovation/

8. http://mccollcenter.org/innovation-institute

9. http://www.1871.com/

10. http://www.chicagoinnovationmentors.org/

About the Author

Stephen A. Di Biase, PhD

Stephen is the president of Premier Insights, LLC, an innovation practices consultancy. He is a member of Cornerstone Angels, a Chicago-based angel investor group. He has served as the Chief Executive Officer of Laser Application Technologies, a high technology company delivering technology to the food service industry. As a current Vistage Chair, he mentors CEOs of technology-based start-ups. In addition, Stephen is an adjunct professor at Benedictine University.

Previously, Stephen served as the Chief Scientific Officer of Elevance Renewable Sciences, a high technology specialty chemicals company, and as the Senior Vice President and Chief Scientific Officer for the Research Development and Engineering Department at Diversey Inc. In these roles he was responsible for technology innovation, research, development efforts, and technical resource management. He also served as interim Senior Vice President of Human Resources.

Before joining JohnsonDiversey, Dr. Di Biase spent 26 years with the Lubrizol Corporation, where he held a variety of leadership positions, including general management roles and Vice President – Research, Development and Engineering and Vice President – Emulsified Products.

He is a 1974 graduate of St. John Fisher College with a Bachelor of Science degree in chemistry and earning a doctorate degree in chemistry from Pennsylvania State University in 1978.

Stephen is also a past member of the Board of Trustees for the Mt. Union College and the Industrial Research Institute, and sits on the Science Advisory Board for The Pennsylvania State University. He has served as chairman of The Lubrizol Foundation Scholarship Committee, Chairman of the Northeastern Ohio Section of the American Chemical Society, Board member of the Cleveland Area Research Directors (CARD) and in The Boy Scouts of America where he served in a variety of posts. Dr. Di Biase has been honored by The Pennsylvania State University College of Science with its 2007 Distinguished Alumni Award. He is also an adjunct professor at Benedictine University and guest lecturer on entrepreneurship and innovation at the Kellogg School of Business at Northwestern University.